You Won't Need That

You Won't Need That

poems by

ROBERT GREGORY

ACME POEM COMPANY
WILLOW SPRINGS EDITIONS
SPOKANE, WASHINGTON

Willow Springs Editions, Spokane, WA 99202
Copyright © 2013 by Robert Gregory
Printed in the United States of America
All Rights Reserved.
Printed by Gray Dog Press.
ISBN-13: 978-0-98-32317-3-8

Cataloguing and Publication Information available from the Library of Congress.

Cover Photo: "Skydiver's Moon" by Trish Mistric
See more of Trish Mistric's photography by visiting her websites:
http://www.redbubble.com/people/pmistric
http://fineartamerica.com/profiles/trish-mistric.html

Author Photo: Keith A. Barker
See more of Keith Barker's photos at http://www.kbarkerphoto.com/

The title for this collection is inspired by Josh Jackson's interview of musical artist Ingrid Jensen,
recorded live April 12, 2012 for WGBO's concert: "Ingrid Jensen Quintet: Live at Berklee
College" (used by permission). Hear Ingrid Jensen's music and interview at http://www.npr.
org/event/music/150361526/ingrid-jensen-quintet-live-at-berklee-concert, as well as her website:
http://www.ingridjensen.com/

Design and Layout: Tim Grassley, Preston Ham, Marie Hoffman, & Dorian Karahalios

First Edition

This and other Willow Springs Editions publications may be viewed online at our website:
http://sites.ewu.edu/wseditions/

for La Poulette

CONTENTS

"It was this same street, a few blocks down, if they still have an ensemble room there, looking out over Boylston Street. It was the first time I'd played free. I showed up with my Bb Real Book and it was kind of embarrassing. Everybody said . . . 'you won't need that . . . we're just going to look out the window and play off what we see.'"

—*Ingrid Jensen*

Open Sky and Running Sky

All the easy secrets gone away, gone off to open
sky, the one with ragged bits of cloud because
the wind was tearing at them all night long:

a bored and lonely dog on bare and dusty space
inside a chain-link fence with kitchen rag, a foot
of sticky rope, a slipper stolen for his play.

Here it comes as running sky, on the way
to somewhere sweet: no cancellation faces now
no random razor lies, no shiny empty riddle.

Instead, the lost and foolish leaves, a sudden slash
of rain to bring their colors up, slow their
sway, gather up their hiss and sigh, clear away
a little space for coming open, just enough

DARK WHERE YOU ARE

Dark where you are now, inside the wandering
the eastern waters
dark, you are moving east
and west with your birds and your women
in a long cloud, in sweet new engines
made for reproduction
where everything can center and reanimate
the weather sultry now, the earth again
as black as when we sat together
all night long to watch the sun go
a black-eyed fox and willows all that
day, the country naked, weather
raw, it rained with violence, two swans
that stayed just out of
gunshot, a range of bleak and barren
hills, a wolf the men consumed
with satisfaction, appearance
of the skinny local rain, a kind of thin intensity
an angry child
eating local earth, we passed a river like
the one where you are
now, gigantic sycamores they had adorned
in former days, wings and long ribbons of skin,
the old men say they have the skill of killing
with their eyes, the stars again
invisible, the water clear and of a green
color, the finding of an old beaten
road to please us, places where fires had
been lately made, and dark where
a cloudy streak along the water, birds fly
through their silence, at the turning
of the final year, transcribing movements
of the breezes in the grass, the boats

all made of paper, ragged mountains coming
up, the local night came
down, near this place a river made the place
the place where you are now
the local night made gestures in the heavy air
the water sent them back with subtle
movements with sweetness, with the name for
what makes changes, turning everything
we thought to have into itself and
then into the dark

THINGS THAT ARE NOT

The winter is an eye, is watching things that are
not as though they were, as once

in Noah's time, in soft and gentle air, they found
him flat on holy ground

imagining the iron doors, the worms and monsters:

Our creatures are our thoughts, the dog—
be sure he knows his grass, knows how to see

these white enraptured places flowering
all our named and lovely shelters

from the wind and winter rain that my
bewildered heart it raises up and spills

Old Miss Death and Her Sister

Above the common region of the clouds
where the lightning is remarkably red
two ladies—it's said they came by longing
there—were wandering above a planet
full of breath

curving and proud, as from another day
as in the solemn discussions of children
ignoring the dog rain and dust rain
entering thereby into a slow and subtle
rapture, talking all night beneath flowering trees

of a spider with a symmetrical web
and the sky and the calm waters, the long thoughts
of the moon, blue glass from an old grave
meant for heathen ornament, saying

let us sit in the garden and
watch the evening pass, watch the
air in its various shapes and modifications:
a word going into itself, fair and beautiful cities
going into silver lines
the noise made by the butterflies
the murmur of ink in its hole, the spirits
living under bridges, a stone that fell
from the upper sky
that burned the branch of a
mulberry tree, scared a cross-eyed possum,
scattered bits of calico and lace, the
shabby dress that old Miss Death goes
around in, around and around in

The Alibi

Sorry I haven't written in so long—
Preoccupied with clouds, she said in her letter,
with seeing a familiar demon in the clouds,
a change of gender in the clouds, irresponsible
and lazy clouds, thinking of having a chance to eat
a whole cloud by herself someday, to marry a cloud
and have little clouds (named Cloudia and
Cloudette), to inhale some clouds and then exhale
them good as new, to know and yet keep secrets
from some clouds, to consider if clouds are naked
or clothed (and if clothed, what they look like nude)
to consider, further, the instant and temporary clouds
the permanent clouds with doors and clean windows
to see the clouds walking like men, or gliding, creeping
dancing, napping, procrastinating, etc., or pretending
to be camels and battleships and fish and mountains
and then thinking of clouds content to be clouds
and nothing else, remembering the last time she was
a cloud herself, or dreamed she kissed a cloud, committed
condensation with a cloud who was tattoo'd with
"caution: cloud is very hot." So naturally she had to think
were Clouds a substitute for people? (as in the parade
before Adam, though he didn't think so). Cloud
as a careless man's companion, a forgetful woman's
friend, or in the catalog of friends elsewhere? With
the geometric friend, the elaborate friend who came with
instructions, the shifting uncharted friend, the gray
and overcast friend, the friend with many shoes
and many jokes, the bare-assed unembarrassed friend
the friend with rational tendencies, the friend in the sky
(always high and blue), the friend made mostly of rain
the friend made of leaves and branches, the friend
held together with thread (the one with big eyes and

a permanent smile), the chocolate friend who hated sun
the friend made of bread who was wonderful fresh
but quickly got stale and then began to turn blue
around the edges, the friend of combed cotton (soft
but full of hidden thorns, long wicked and black)
the scraped and worn-down friend who knew all the
troubles there were and had survived them, the plush
and silky friend who didn't, the friend with extra teeth,
the gloomy friend with nice ankles (but unaware of that)
the friend disguised as a pine tree sometimes, the friend
disguised as an enemy, the friend with sore places
that never heal, the invisible friend who's helpful even so
the friend in a box (a handsome one), the unpainted friend
who lacks primer, the neutral friend who needs a little salt,
the hairless friend who worries about hair returning someday
the butterfly friend and her friend the unshakable (yours?)

17

TRANSLATION

What is all this exactly? For instance—
cutting the blue off the edge
of the bread, pulling the tab on a can,
asking the cat about her nocturnal
adventures, listening to voices prate
about Ghana and GM, getting used to
being vertical and subject to gravity
again, blinking in the porcelain glare
(the spirits are hiding in the trees
and the trees are moving and stirring)
greeting the growly but friendly young
man in the cafeteria, brushing away
insects of dream or disaggregated memory
or dreaming they are being brushed
away instead of respun (the spirits are)
relocated, nominated, set to work—

Yes, morning, more or less: the offices
still dark and quiet, the square still empty.
A white 150 silently appears: the girl
from the service to water the plants.
The feral cat who hunts this space for
a living slips past about her solitary
business, the lines of her body radiate
a subtle & beautiful thought. The dangling
branches of wisteria shift and shiver, they
tremble, they rise and they fall as a
way to translate what the breezes
are saying as they pass in and out of
each other and all this whatever it is

THE CENTRAL SECRET

is to be inside the rush and spat of birdsong, in the sun
came up and went away, in the rags and baby dolls inside
a dirty yard, inside the small dry spiders hiding them away
from winter's hands, inside a dusty kitchen where
the roasting chicken smells like gin, across the faded
pages where he talks of journeys done for pickery
that then become a cruel and handsome empire, and
this labyrinth as well of rivers, broken islands, an
easterly wind, a wound received from nowhere
long-lasting forms of mind, old papers torn and
scattered by digital rats, a salt place where the deer
come down to the waterside as the light gets more
and more skittish, a lady whom the time
surprised with sorrow, inside a long slow pass
across the meadow, a single silver drone as it circles
and turns, the rasp of a mockingbird, the sound
of an eager young rain, which is (all is) to be inside

Again Maybe

Scattered among the fancy girls here and there,
crossing the river seated on a feather now
a clever one, a silly one, a sly one, who could say?

The ripples catching the light on their backs

"Let us remember that everything is
double," he wrote and stopped to consider:
was it really?

The wind was high and told her secrets:
the dogs, high grass, a rusting car, that the sun
is held and fascinated, the moon
immaculate, goes through in easy
knife, etc.

The gossip said she swapped her mother
to the muskrats in return for a thicket
of the best raspberries; the story says
that in among the trees, a girl who looked
like her had slept for twenty years
protected from the moonlight
by courteous bears

The tiny ferryman and his hairy sons
began as soon as they saw her walking
barefoot to the landing

They're singing about those foolish
things again, Father, she said
to the grumpy bear with the walking stick,
but smiling despite herself
Not much of an answer, the wind thought,
I'll try her again; but the rain (another
fancy girl) was like why bother?

St. Anthony's Pig Goes South

The old shepherd's big visible bones
attracting a beautiful crow because of old
symmetry, of two and then three right
angles in these flat and filthy days, and a
small and clever blue animal as well—
St. Anthony's pig as seen in all the pictures
of the man himself, down in the left-
hand corner that followed everywhere
despite the strange adventure of
the bloody spirits with the hanging beards
along I-95, walking stiff, declaiming,
ignoring the brush of bird shadow, the lasting
indifference and delicate breath from
inside the loblolly pines, the stare
of a wandering fox a green and confident eye
avoiding the silly white faces in houses in
yet another careful and worrisome
time, the steady lights that still burn on in the
daytime, a sharp and subtle wind
advancing with its information

Gloss (The Other Kind) Is Lacking

To give the sense of green mornings,
one not made of words but like a homemade

paper boat drifting on a weedy spiral
creek, moving into

rain that taps against true surfaces,
into small and daily mysteries: dock and

henbit and Joe Pye weed in neglected
places in a small unprosperous town lost

in a vast uneasy busy nation, on a continent

riding a smiling monster, rolling through
a black and empty is-because-it-is

DIME

A deep and heavy black at first, and so it's bright
& blazing out: a brand new tin can moon. And
then an hour later with the gray adulterating all that
black, it's more like something left out in the sun
too long and fading, just a flat and rounded place
among the curved and thin, the pulled and twisted
and elaborated elongated clouds, a dime someone
has dropped while reaching for the car keys with
arms full of groceries, head full of staged imaginary
conversations, inaudible to others but loud enough
internally to drown the sound of a small and shiny
moon that strikes the creamy blacktop edgeways and
then is wobbling and tipping over, falling face-first
holding still, breathing, sleeping.

And then the other light begins, the one that reddens
all the trees along their sleeping borderlines and is
an enemy to moon continuation, the light that glitters
and advances in the wreckage of the dew: someone
has dropped their load, it shattered and went everywhere,
there's way too much to stoop and gather up, they've
gone away and left it here. That's the light that makes
the shadows move out slowly from the trees without
a word, it shows itself in complicated crisscross places
where the spiders have been working in the grass, that
endless thin and shining substance drawn out from
themselves (a kind of conversation less imaginary but
that's linked to groceries all the same) and now the
birds are wandering and hunting in the day's new grass
which seems to happen over and over and over, on
Monday mornings especially (though they would
disagree respectfully, they'd say it's never quite the
same because the seasons and the weather and the things

the humans do all change the taste of it and feel of it
and span of change of it from darkening to day and
change what's there to hunt and all the tastes and
movements of the things as well: just think of how the
greenhead flies and fat old whiskered bees in hairy
overcoats move staggering and drunk some days
like someone just up out of bed and dropping
without noticing the images and words from
dreams the way a tree will drop its seeds to spin on
down and then its leaves to spin the same way later on
not even partly conscious of all this, on his way into
the kitchen for the making of coffee, stepping sideways
and regaining balance with his arms out like a man
become a tree temporarily and as if the once familiar
tile has changed into a wire in a circus act high up
above the ground above the lions, crabby on their
hassocks and the ladies in flesh-colored tights and
spangles, showing big and repeated broad elaborate
exaggerated curving smiles while all the children cheer
and clap and beg for dimes to give the peanut man
dimes a few of them will drop and lose and then
remember, some of them, much later, on an otherwise
ordinary morning)

STILL EARLY

Still early so the
moon's gone back up
to the house,
uneaten fireflies and
stars ignore each
other as they
fade, an early witch
is late, is muttering and
looking for her other
shoe in the black
and blue grass,
and the lovely word
goes off unnoticed
through the
black arrangements
of this space, which comes
back here to rest (a lost
feather) lightly on
the empty
parking lots, the grass
hungover from
a day of rain, the fat
and easy days to
come, the
long unspoken hours
passing steadily away like
clouds in careful
sentences, moving eastward
one by one, folded in and
blurred along their
boundaries, above the vehicles
that run in one direction
now and things about
to open for a time

PROPOSAL

> The Rose is out of town.
>
> *—Emily Dickinson*

After days of Spangle Rain, the Crickets folded
in the Weeds began to sing a Lewd Request,
both Minimal and repetitious, just as it Should be.

Everything in this is just "a Waste of Time," said
all the Panelists. Whatever Time might be.
It could be Bad. Consider it.

Asking for a mystery ride along the Mystery
Road? Asking for Excited Blaze to put its
pointy tongue on all portentous Archives and
pretentious Ledgers, gobbling and flickering
till everything

we like to call "The Past" has been Consumed?
Legerdemain. Along with everything called "Visions"
(every little co. can have one now) and then a box
Someone had put up on the shelf and marked
"Important – Keep"?

Recommend we Fund. But that Means
everything is to be Gone to make an outcome:
Swaying Shadows: Deliverables: deliverance.

So Now what? said the Smoke. Are we Gone?

A School for Silence

To the smaller insects, trees
are gods: huge, benevolent,

abstracted. The wind exaggerates
the yellow of her dress. Halfway and

partial regrets, neatly bisected:
some for now and some

for later. The light is curious and
mild. A school
for silence

MADE OF GRASS

On a frozen shepherd, shoes he made of grass
the smell of cigarettes and drying hay
the insect delighted by sweat, people in a run of
small troubles, I have heard the old men
say in early light the colors of the trees seem
darker still, the clatter of the wooden swords
and the shouts of the players, a phantom
well-known in the town appeared to Dr.
Turberville's sister, in September when the rain
becomes elliptical, the spies appear in clouds
and trees, a burned up sky is opening,
three hundred golden bees were sighted, our
daily blood, our daily breath, a small green bottle
made for tears, the plump white fingers of
the one they like to say is Cynthia, her tiny handful
of days, the birds around the spotlights
catching moths, along the dirty road
of dreams and able now at last to be the rain,
interior and secret virtues, nothing
visible in these pretended heavens but the
names in torn arrangement, under the fall of
the wind, at the turning and falling of the days

To the east, a feather of new cloud the trees have
snagged and the wind wants to take and shred,
and then examine. Swallows dive, then curve and
rise. Soon is winter in a long curve. The thing
we live on blue as dragon's bone and floating
out in nowhere. Leaves hang down. A tang of rain

A STRANGER

A daylit moon, very small and crisp, wandered in
from somewhere just to illustrate the phrase the
other world. Touch of a chill in the weightless air
odd and sudden, soft and milky light, and then
a breeze jumps up and runs, as sharp as winter is
the leaves all tremble and sigh as she rushes
by, ghost of Helen still a kid, or some young
Queen-to-be just out of storybooks, come to see
the bayonets, watch the silly buildings going up

This Paper City Now

No resistance in this paper city now,
no anticipation, staring like a child with
an old nature, South a bad direction then
the winter mainly rain, but they had a
sweeter angel in their music, here
the smaller day comes on, you see the places
underneath the trees grow long and dark
the grass begins to curve beneath its weight
of dew, in the newer more assertive light
a young beast on its own in the glittering field
and in the town the wind patrolling empty streets
resolved spirits in a green retreat and in and
out among the ordinary, a pretty little beast
a melancholy dream, desire takes its rest
for now, though every man is pestered
by imaginary pleasures, bold as beggars
in position down along the lateral streets
in the doorways, in the dirty faces of the buildings
as the world was torn, an unfortunate hour
the light beginning to go, now the color
of a yellow weed the dyers use, a pretty little
beast is drawn to its fragrance, they say

DUST AND AGGREGATION

Out of which comes almost anything, say: Flash as Robin
Hood, the pointy-beard professor at the wheel, needles
jumping while they both pretend to care, the rocket just a
trick, a toy with lazy languid sparks to signify combustion
but we didn't know the difference yet and elsewhere quantum
physics flew around inside the heads of other strange

professors while Flash went after foreigners in outer space:
Ming the Merciless, his Fu Manchu mustache to signify
inscrutable, on Planet X the Mud Men, pieces of the barren
hills until they pulled away and started walking. In Missouri
in those days the hemp was everywhere, overgrown, left
over from the war, easy for the Basie band to spot even from

the highway and stop to harvest. Where was Bill Monroe
meanwhile? On the way to gig somewhere, cowboy hat
down over his eyes (nowhere safe to put it anyway),
listening (Bluegrass Express a steady buzz and sway on little
two-lane roads) to whatever they could get, the stations
fading in and out: Farm & Fun Time, the Mound City Blue

Blowers from a hotel ballroom in Tulsa, Lem and cronies
at the general store entangled in another funny small town fix,
the reverend doctor so-and-so and choir (hefty ladies,
sounded like, the rev himself as well) *re*
the little black train, snatches of light opera, then the
Philharmonic straight from New York City also known as

Babylon, all cut through with patter, pitches for spring
tonics versus lazy blood, laxatives, half the country
all stopped up, the Carter family guaranteed to do
a family show, no smut, no Bill from Louisville
singing about his lollipop, now and then the news,

what the Italians are up to in Ethiopia, the farm
report, hogs on the Chicago market going for
x cents a pound, keep them and feed them up or let
them go the question every day, and by the side
of the road, a bum in a dirty fedora with his
thumb out, Krishna with a thousand mouths, the dead
go pouring in and pouring in, the boys just don't
have room for him, might be a good chauffeur,
or just some drunken Indian, so they flashed on by
no idea why he had that smile or why he didn't
mind eating their dust

ELEGY IN ADVANCE

Sometimes the moon shines green
above a dirty house
where glims and flickers of a foolish thought
go wandering and
smiling, cigarette girl in a 40's
black-and-white
and large slow-moving stars are blue and
blurred, forgetful.

Then a day when
skinny dogs and old discarded
fantasies are dreaming in the grass in
daylight, elongated and relaxed
and over them the sky
is open wide and perfect up beyond
the rain, and on the sidewalk
there's a puddle newly
formed to demonstrate the evidence for
the other place: that duplicated sky

Be Motion

The delicate hiss of the morning, bewildered
insect on the new floor, holding still, all

directions now the same, the people likewise
naked like their alphabet, moving in the

push and slide, the daily delicate

today a smudge, a cloud
to make a line of trees be motion

long knuckled grass and weeds go limp
under solitary rain and busy families of rain

the river's coils continue uncorrected,
ignore the angularity of the day, the dirt

is distance, the delicate is depth and surface
the estuary's gray, a film of salt

an instant, then another
unstable not so bad when it's

all burning anyway

EDGE

The sweet and subtle day
a sky unfolded by the chill

Red thighs of the houses
a sparrow busy in the wet grass

Chairs with beautiful curves
a girl with a smile full of bones and silk

Vague shapes of old mountains,
worn down, domesticated

Blaze of a bird in a bare tree
on the far edge of winter, sound of
the spatter of rain

THIS GREAT BIG GRACEFUL AND LOPSIDED PERSONAGE OR MOON

A rabbit the size of my fist or yours or anyone's
Sheets on a line lifted by the wind for no reason

He dug with his whole body and still I didn't smell a thing
The wind doesn't live here any more, the old woman liked to say

The flowers had a dirty glow
Her smile meant trouble for someone and herself as well

The wind is teasing the leaves
The day is teasing the stiff dignified buildings

This long easy drift is what they all wished for and now it's here again
From corners of the body: reports on surfaces and shapes

The axe bites into wood, the white space opens up
No names on the headstones, a pleasant part of the dream

Another is the entrance of the splayfoot queen, her radiance

CAUTIONARY TALE

On the day's page, the buildings blank as yet,
faint investigation of the skin by an early breeze

in a bare time and over there a hungry animal
is now holding very still amid what will soon be

the glow of new grass in new light. Head
tucked in well back. One visible eye as black

as the black all around it or even more so. Careful
angle of the long and fragile ears (signifying

caution). It can come at any time. Compacting
itself, pretending to be a flower, a letter in an

ancient alphabet, a creature in a primer standing
very still above something sensible and ready

to be memorized in two or maybe four of those
thin morbid homely lines about the common end

with rhymes that thud and clump along like the
boots of a weary man, night watchman, say, who's

been walking and walking his rounds and finally
is home, walking upstairs—bare, uncarpeted,

in a hallway with a bare light burning up above—
toward his once new and now quite empty bed

NAMELESS

Seeds of sleep have worked up
to the surface. In places
where the word is easy-come,
the boat is rocking for no
reason, the evening
behaving, the moon inspects
the residue of snakeish day: the over-
clarified and classified, the wind
just going up and down, the
easy rush of birds obscured by
the punctuated lady, the
articulated man. One cloud, last
long angle of light

In the Lovely Dark Again

In the lovely dark about to leave,
love-crazy repetition songs from little things
are leaving off, a wicked breeze begins
to shift and rearrange the leaves who'd rather

lie in repetitious crowds, in whispering, in
telling lies identically about the slow return
but no, it's pushing them to flip and hunch
and scratch their way across the road and back
again and then again until another slender
unassuming day kicks in, a slow and eastward

slide of clouds and secret subatomic forces
falling through the sleepy world, invisible and blue

ACKNOWLEDGEMENTS

The author wishes to thank the editors of the following print and electronic publications in which some of these poems first appeared:

Raritan: "Edge" and "Cautionary Tale"

Hanging Loose: "Dime," "A Stranger," "Translation," "Again Maybe," and "The Alibi"

Caliban: "Proposal"

Gargoyle: "Elegy in Advance"

ACME POEM COMPANY

Willow Springs Editions is a small literary press housed in Eastern Washington University's Inland Northwest Center for Writers in Spokane. Its annual chapbook series selects and publishes contemporary surrealist poetry under the auspices of the Acme Poem Company.

PREVIOUS COLLECTIONS

Ray Amorosi, *Gnawing on a Thin Man*

Adam Hammer, *No Time for Dancing*

For a complete list of selections from Willow Springs Editions and ordering information, visit:

http://sites.ewu.edu/wseditions/

Willow Springs Editions staff contributors to this book: Jaime Baird, LeAnn Bjerken, Casey M. Fowler, Tim Grassley, Preston Ham, Marie Hoffman, Merideth Jeffries, Dorian Karahalios, Tim Pringle, Cat Sarytchoff, Kati Stunkard, and Holly Weiler.